D1527285

MARY A.J.

Triumph Over Tragedy

A Journey of Healing, Faith, and Forgiveness

Give
THANKS
to the *Lord*
for He is good; His love endures forever.
–1 Chronicles 16:34

Copyright © 2024 by Mary A.J.

All rights reserved. No part of this publication may be reproduced, stored or transmitted in any form or by any means, electronic, mechanical, photocopying, recording, scanning, or otherwise without written permission from the publisher. It is illegal to copy this book, post it to a website, or distribute it by any other means without permission.

Mary A.J. asserts the moral right to be identified as the author of this work.

Mary A.J. has no responsibility for the persistence or accuracy of URLs for external or third-party Internet Websites referred to in this publication and does not guarantee that any content on such Websites is, or will remain, accurate or appropriate.

Designations used by companies to distinguish their products are often claimed as trademarks. All brand names and product names used in this book and on its cover are trade names, service marks, trademarks and registered trademarks of their respective owners. The publishers and the book are not associated with any product or vendor mentioned in this book. None of the companies referenced within the book have endorsed the book.

First edition

This book was professionally typeset on Reedsy.
Find out more at reedsy.com

This book is dedicated to my siblings, all six of them, and those I have yet to meet. You have shaped my life in ways words can scarcely express.

To those enduring any form of abuse, may this book serve as a beacon of hope and a reminder that you are not alone. I dedicate this to the survivors, the fighters, and those still searching for their way out. Your strength is unparalleled, even on the days when you may not feel it.

Special Considerations

All thoughts expressed here are my own, except for information sourced from the National Domestic Abuse Center, Bassett Healthcare Network, my sister, and my brother.

Contents

II Part II

Foreword

Life often presents us with challenges that test the very core of who we are. In the face of pain, loss, and adversity, we are given a choice: to allow our struggles to define us or to rise above them with courage, faith, and resilience. Mary: A Journey of Healing and Faith *invites us into a powerful story of transformation, one that resonates with anyone who has ever felt the weight of pain or the burden of unhealed wounds.*

This book is more than a collection of experiences; it is a guide for those seeking to confront their deepest hurts and embark on a journey toward healing. Mary's story is one of vulnerability, strength, and ultimately, hope. It is through her struggles that she discovered the profound truth that healing is not a destination but a continuous journey—one that requires faith, patience, and a willingness to embrace vulnerability.

Throughout these pages, you will find yourself walking

alongside Mary as she confronts the emotional toll of pain, breaks through denial, and surrenders to the process of healing. Her insights into the role of faith, the importance of forgiveness, and the power of vulnerability offer valuable lessons for anyone seeking to rebuild their lives after heartache.

I encourage you to read this book not only with an open mind but with an open heart. Let Mary's story inspires you to look within, to confront your own pain, and to trust that healing is possible. As you read, you may find yourself reminded of the words of Isaiah 40:31: "But those who hope in the Lord will renew their strength. They will soar on wings like eagles; they will run and not grow weary; they will walk and not be faint."

May this book serve as a beacon of light on your own journey of healing, guiding you toward peace, faith, and the courage to embrace new beginnings. At the end, she triumphs in Yeshua's name.

With hope and faith,

Chimene Castor, P.h.D

Acknowledgments

To all the brave survivors of domestic violence, I want to reach out with heartfelt compassion and remind you that you are not alone on this journey.

Your strength and resilience inspire us all, and it's important to acknowledge the courage it takes to face each day. Healing is a process that unfolds in its own time, but please hold onto the hope that brighter days are ahead.

Trust God and trust yourself, and know that seeking support from those who care is not only okay but a vital step towards your well-being. You are deserving of love, respect, and a life filled with peace and joy.

Stay strong and remember, you are never alone.

I

Part I

Overcoming the Pain of Domestic Violence

One

Chapter 1: The Struggle for Survival

Growing up, home was both a place of familiarity and fear. On the surface, our family seemed respectable. My father had a reputation in the community for being a hardworking man, and our family appeared to have it all together. But behind those closed doors, it was a different story. My father's temper and alcoholism ruled our household, and as a child, I often felt trapped in a place that was supposed to be my haven.

One of the hardest things for me was the unpredictability of it all. I never knew what would set my father off, or when a peaceful evening would turn into a night of shouting and violence. I lived with constant anxiety, always waiting for the next explosion. At a young age, I thought I had to carry that burden alone. I didn't know how to ask for help, and I wasn't sure if anyone could understand the pain and fear I felt.

As a child, I didn't realize how important it was to seek help when living in a situation of abuse. I kept everything inside, hiding my pain because I thought that's what I was supposed to do. But now, looking back, I know that staying silent only deepened my wounds.

Abuse is a heavy burden, and no one should have to bear it alone. It's so important to reach out, to talk to someone, whether it's a trusted family member, a friend, or a professional. There is no shame in seeking help. In fact, it's one of the bravest things a person can do.

I also learned that trusting in God is essential when facing the pain of abuse. Even when I couldn't see a way out, God was there, ready to guide me toward healing. I remember crying out to Him in the darkness, praying for an escape, for peace. It didn't come right away, but over time, I learned to trust that God had a plan for me. He was leading me to safety, to freedom, even when I didn't realize it. God promises that He will never leave us in our suffering. He is always there, and we must trust that He will provide a way out. *"No temptation has overtaken you except what is common to mankind. And God is faithful; he will not let you be tempted beyond what you can bear. But when you are tempted, he will also provide a way out so that you can endure it."* — *1 Corinthians 10:13 (NIV)*

This verse reminds me that God is always working, even in the hardest moments. He doesn't abandon us in our pain. Instead, He walks with us, providing the strength we need to endure and guiding us to the help we need. Trusting God is the key to finding peace, even in the darkest times.

I now realize how important it is to lean on the support of others and to trust that God will lead us to safety. The journey out of abuse is not an easy one, but with God's help and the right support, it is possible. We must take that first step and ask for help, trusting that God will carry us through.

The Lord is my rock, my fortress and my deliverer; my God is my rock, in whom I take refuge, my shield and the horn of my salvation, my stronghold." — Psalm 18:2 (NIV)

Prayer for Protection and Guidance

Lord, in the moments of fear and uncertainty, be my fortress and my refuge. Help me to find the courage to seek help when I am in pain and give me the strength to trust in Your plan for my life. Guide me to the people and resources that will help me heal and remind me that I am never alone. Protect me and show me the way out, Lord, just as You have promised.

In Yeshua's name, Amen.

Two

Chapter 2: Journey Through Darkness

Living through darkness was not something I ever expected to face as a child. I didn't have the words to explain what was happening in my home or the emotions I carried with me every day. There were times when it felt like I was just existing—barely surviving.

The present, at that time, felt like a battlefield, filled with fear, confusion, and pain. I was constantly in survival mode, and for years, I didn't even realize it. I was just trying to get through each day, doing whatever I could to stay safe, to avoid the next outburst, to make it through another night. Looking back, I can see that survival mode was not living—it was just enduring. But at the time, it was all I knew.

The Silent Struggle: Living in Survival Mode

When you're living in survival mode, everything feels like a threat. I remember being hyper-aware of every sound, every movement in the house. The creak of the floorboards, the opening of a door, the clinking of a glass—these were the sounds that could mean the difference between peace and chaos. As a child, I didn't understand why I felt so anxious all the time. I thought this was just the way life was. I was constantly on edge, always preparing for the worst.

Living in survival mode took a toll on my body and my soul. I felt exhausted, even though I was just a child. It's a kind of tiredness that goes beyond physical exhaustion. It was like my spirit was worn out, constantly bracing for impact, never knowing when the next storm would come. I withdrew into myself, isolating my emotions because I thought that was the only way to protect myself. But I was wrong—survival mode kept me trapped in a cycle of fear and hopelessness.

"Even though I walk through the darkest valley, I will fear no evil, for you are with me; your rod and your staff, they comfort me." — Psalm 23:4 (NIV)

God's promise to walk with me through the darkest valleys is something I didn't understand back then, but looking back, I know He was with me. Even in the middle of the chaos, He was guiding me, comforting me in ways I couldn't see at the time.

Battling Feelings of Worthlessness

One of the most difficult things to cope with, as I grew older, was the sense of worthlessness that came from living in an abusive environment. The words spoken in anger, the violence that seemed to erupt out of nowhere—it all chipped away at my sense of self. I began to believe that maybe I wasn't worthy of love or happiness. I internalized those messages, thinking that if I was different, maybe the violence would stop. Maybe if I was better, everything would be okay.

But that's the thing about abuse—it makes you believe lies. It makes you believe that you're not enough, that you're flawed, that somehow you deserve the pain. These feelings of worthlessness stayed with me for years, long after the abuse ended. It's a struggle that many survivors face—the battle to reclaim their self-worth, to believe that they are loved, that they matter.

"You are precious and honored in my sight, and because I love you, I will give people in exchange for you, nations in exchange for your life." — Isaiah 43:4 (NIV)

This verse has been a lifeline for me. To know that I am precious in God's sight, that He sees me as worthy of love and honor—that truth is something I must remind myself of daily. God's love is not conditional, and it's not based on how others treat me. His love declares my value, even when I can't see it for myself.

Finding God's Presence in the Chaos

In the middle of all that darkness, it was hard to see God's presence. As a child, I often wondered if He had forgotten about me. I prayed for the pain to go away, but it didn't. And so, I began to question if God was there, if He cared about me at all. But now, looking back, I can see how He was present, even in the chaos. He was there in the moments of peace, in the unexpected acts of kindness, in the strength I didn't know I had.

There were times when I would catch a glimpse of hope—a kind word from a neighbor, a teacher who cared, or a moment of quiet when I could escape into a book or a song. These were small blessings, but they were God's way of showing me that I wasn't alone. Even when I couldn't feel Him, He was there, guiding me through the storm.

"Be still and know that I am God; I will be exalted among the nations, I will be exalted in the earth." — Psalm 46:10 (NIV)

The call to "be still" is something I've come to appreciate as I've gotten older. It's in the stillness that I've found God's presence most clearly. When life feels overwhelming, it's the moments of stillness, the pauses in the chaos, where I can hear God's voice reminding me that He is in control.

Survival Skills: Steps to Survive and Thrive

Surviving abuse is one thing, but I know now that God doesn't just want us to survive—He wants us to thrive. It took me a long time to realize that I was allowed to hope for more than just survival. I had to learn new ways of thinking, new ways of living, and most importantly, I had to learn to ask for help. There were a few key things that helped me on my journey toward healing:

Seeking Support: I learned that I couldn't do it alone. Whether it was through counseling, friends, or a church community, I needed people to walk with me through the healing process. Isolation only deepened the wounds.

Developing a Prayer Life: Prayer became my lifeline. I didn't always have the words to pray, but just sitting in God's presence, pouring out my heart, gave me strength. I learned that prayer wasn't just about asking for things—it was about finding comfort in God's presence.

Setting Boundaries: I had to learn to set boundaries with the people in my life, even family. I realized that protecting my peace was important, and sometimes that meant creating distance from toxic relationships.

Finding Joy in Small Moments: One of the hardest things was learning to find joy again. For so long, I had been focused on just getting through the day. But as I healed, I began to see that joy could be found even in the smallest moments—a sunrise, a cup of tea, a conversation with a friend. These moments of joy became my lifeline, reminding me that life is still beautiful, even after pain.

"I can do all things through Christ who strengthens me." — **Philippians 4:13 (NKJV)**

With Christ's strength, I learned that I could do more than just survive. I could thrive. I could reclaim my life, my joy, and my future. It wasn't easy, and there are still days when the past feels heavy, but I know that with God's help, I can overcome anything.

Prayer for Strength to Endure

Heavenly Father,

I feel overwhelmed by the struggles of today. I ask that You give me the strength to endure and the courage to move forward. Help me to trust in Your presence even when I cannot see it and remind me that You are my refuge. Guide me through this season of difficulty and lead me to a place of peace and hope.

Teach me to find joy, even in the small moments, and help me to know that I am loved and worthy.

In Yeshua's name, Amen.

Three

Chapter 3: The Confusing Duality of My Father

As a child, trying to understand my father was like trying to solve a puzzle with missing pieces. On some days, he was everything I thought a father should be—responsible, hard-working, and even admired by the people around us. Those were the days I loved him deeply. I could see the good in him, the man who provided for our family, the man who insisted that we go to church, do well in school, and behave respectfully. When he was sober, he had a sharp mind, a good business sense, and even a sense of humor that made him enjoyable to be around.

But then, there were other days—days that felt like they came out of nowhere—when the drinking would take over. It was as if he became a completely different person, someone I didn't recognize and didn't know how to love. The alcohol transformed him into someone with a temper that seemed uncontrollable. The laughter and smiles would disappear, replaced by yelling, harsh words, and sometimes even worse. It wasn't just his actions that changed—it was his entire demeanor. His eyes would darken, his posture would stiffen, and his voice would become something I dreaded.

As a child, this duality was incredibly confusing. One moment, he was the father I could look up to, and the next, he was the man I feared most. Living in a home with that kind of unpredictability created a constant state of anxiety in me. I never knew which version of him I would get. Would he be the father who cared, or the man who seemed consumed by anger? I remember the feeling of dread that would creep over me whenever I heard his voice after a night of drinking. I would brace myself, hoping that he wouldn't lash out, but never being sure what would happen next.

It was hard to reconcile these two versions of my father. I felt torn between loving him and resenting him. On the days when he was kind, when he acted like the father, I needed him to be, I wanted to believe that this was who he really was—that the drinking was just an unfortunate part of his life that didn't define him. But then the rage would come, and I couldn't help but wonder if the anger, the temper, and the cruelty were his true nature.

Often, we found me wondering how you could love someone who caused so much pain. How could we reconcile to the father who made sure we had food on the table with the man who would shout and scare us when the alcohol took over? I wanted so badly to respect him because I knew that was what I was supposed to do as his child. I wanted to honor him because he was my father. But his actions made it almost impossible to give him the respect that he demanded.

One of the hardest things for me as a child was not understanding why he was like this. I couldn't figure out why he would be so good on some days and so terrifying on others. It made me question everything. Was it something I had done? Was I somehow responsible for his anger? If I behaved better, would he stop drinking? These were the thoughts that plagued me as a child. I didn't have the emotional tools to process what was happening, so I did what many children do—I blamed myself.

I remember many nights lying in bed, feeling a mixture of fear and confusion. I wanted to love my father, but I didn't know how to love someone who caused so much damage. I felt guilty for the resentment that grew inside me, but I also felt angry that I had to deal with this. No child should have to navigate the complexities of loving someone who is both a provider and a source of trauma. But that was my reality.

As I grew older, I began to understand that my father's actions were not my fault. His drinking, his temper, and his unpredictable behavior had nothing to do with me. It took years for me to fully grasp this truth. For so long, I had internalized his actions, thinking that if I could just be better, smarter, or more obedient, then maybe he would stop drinking. But none of that was true. His actions were a result of his own pain, his own struggles, and they had nothing to do with me.

It's taken me even longer to understand that loving someone doesn't mean excusing their behavior. I've learned that it's possible to love someone and still hold them accountable for the pain they've caused. I've come to realize that my love for my father doesn't mean I have to condone his actions. It doesn't mean I have to ignore the damage he caused. Love is complicated, especially when it's intertwined with pain. But I've also learned that love, when rooted in truth, can coexist with boundaries, accountability, and forgiveness.

Reconciling the love and pain I feel toward my father is still a process. Some days, I feel a deep sense of compassion for him, understanding that his own demons—his drinking, his inability to cope with life—were at the root of his behavior. Other days, the hurt feels fresh, and it's harder to extend grace. But I've learned to allow myself to feel both love and pain without guilt. I've learned that it's okay to hold space for both.

God has helped me see that my father's actions were never a reflection of my worth. I am loved, I am valuable, and I didn't deserve the hurt that was caused. That understanding has been the key to my healing. And while forgiveness is a journey, I am grateful that God is walking with me every step of the way.

"Fathers, do not embitter your children, or they will become discouraged." — **Colossians 3:21 (NIV)**

Prayer for Healing from Confusion

Dear Lord God,

Lord, help me to reconcile the love and pain I feel toward my father. Heal the parts of my heart that were hurt by his actions and guide me in how to honor him while acknowledging the hurt he caused. Show me how to set healthy boundaries while extending the love that You have called me to give.

Give me peace during my confusion and show me the path to forgiveness. Let me trust in Your plan, knowing that You are the ultimate healer.

In Yeshua's name Amen.

Four

Chapter 4: My Siblings—My Silent Protectors

As I sit here reflecting on the journey, my sister has taken to share her story, I'm struck by how deeply she has opened her heart in these pages. Growing up as the youngest of seven children, her experiences with our father were both a reflection of and a contrast to the challenges my siblings and I faced. I didn't want to be a lone ranger, only expressing my own thoughts and emotions without considering others. So, I reached out to one of my sister and brother, inviting them to share their stories.

In my sister's word

- *"Even though life in the world as a whole was much better in the 60's and 70's when we were growing up (excluding the racism)*

17

sometimes it was chaotic at our home; because our father was
plagued with the disease of alcoholism that went on for most
of our lines until we were grown and out of the house. So we
experienced some hungry days as well as some sleepless nights.
He waws two different people with very different personalities.
Sometimes, he was a man that the whole community respected
because he had a good business head; and would help various
neighbors with different things and the next day he could be
totally different after he had his dose of gin. He would quickly
turn from Dr. Jekyll to Mr. Hyde.

- It was a very confusing and hard time. Thank God our strong
  Mother made it as close to normal as she could when he wasn't
  violent.

-

- The violence was almost normal in our little neighborhood. Most
  of the men would drink and come home out of control. The
  strange thing was, no matter how out of control daddy got; our
  mom would never allow us to disrespect him as our father. He
  demanded us to always be respectful , get our school work, bring
  good report card home, go to church. He also sent us on the
  citizenship tours. So I guess you could say those things made us
  have some great memories. NO matter how embarrassing things
  would get; sometimes we were considered one of the respectables
  scholastically smart families in the community because of our
  mother's strength and daddy's strictness.

-

- It was always so funny and irritating to me how he insisted
  on us acting with dignity even when he was staggering up and

down the street inebriated!! I guess you must have to live and be
raised in that era and community to understand how we dealt
with it and survived, still loving and respecting our dad.

•

• It is definitely easy a lot of the times; but because we were raised
knowing and believing God, we came through to adulthood in
one piece and with our sanity.Although, we always tease each
other saying we all are a little "touched" and need some "therapy",
but glory to God, all seven of us are still here and wonderfully
blessed in spite of ourselves in Jesus' name and his wonderful
grace and mercy"

In the word of My Brother:

• wow, thinking on it, I think that I need to write a book myself, in
sharing my story, take from it what you want from this. Being
the last of seven children and six years younger than my next
sibling I image my childhood experience was somewhat different
from my siblings. Looking back comparatively, I didn't feel
poor and don't recall wanting for much. We didn't often have
cabinets and refrigerators full of food, but we had a mother that
always made a way. As the saying goes, something from nothing.
Although our community and home were dysfunctional in so
many ways, it was also a village, our father was a mixed bag of
chips, so to speak, He was prideful, somewhat respected in the
community, hard-working man that remained in the household
for all our lives. He also was an abuser, alcoholic and womanizer,
looking back I felt that I was the most protected.

•

• One would think growing up in a home where domestic violence, *alcoholism and unfaithfulness were often the current events, the children would experience trauma that would cause years of depression, phobias and anxieties. Maybe it did. Maybe, I did not fully understand the effect as our culture didn't embrace therapy and mental health. We just dealt with it, mostly by suppressing the negative. However, I feel that the trauma didn't touch me as much for many reasons. I was young, approximately eight and nice when the domestic violence and drinking ceased.*

- *I had a strong humble and protective mother, who did not allow us to verbally or physically disrespect our father, regardless of his many transgressions. I was also blessed with intelligent, caring and influential older siblings that provided positive examples.*

- *Finally, as dysfunctional as the mining community of Muscoda may have been, it also was a caring and spiritual village that produced many success-ful and productive adults.*

Finding Hope in Healing

As one of the older siblings, I took on the role of protector, trying to shield my younger siblings from the storm that brewed within our home. Our father's temper was unpredictable, darkened further by alcoholism, casting a shadow over our lives. For my younger siblings, we created moments of peace amidst the chaos, hoping they wouldn't see or feel the turmoil surrounding us. In those difficult years, hope was hard to come by. But we learned to rely on the quiet reassurance within ourselves—the affirmation that we were more than our circumstances. To reach the future, I knew I had to let go of the hurt from my past.

Looking back, I remember the ways we tried to protect her:

creating stories, playing games, and filling the silence with laughter. We thought that was enough to keep the darkness at bay, that by sparing her from the worst, we could give her a semblance of a normal childhood. But as I read their reflections now, I realize they carried their own silent burden, sensing the strain even if they didn't fully understand it at the time. Their stores of their own pain; it is one of resilience—a testament to the strength that arises when you face the shadows of your past. I am immensely proud of my sibling's courage to share their experiences, and I hope their words bring comfort and strength to others on similar journeys.

As an adult, I reflect on the weight we bore for each other. We were each other's unspoken guardians, silently standing in the gap. Despite the cold words, raised voices, and sometimes the sting of physical violence, we created a fragile sanctuary of love and laughter. Those moments of joy were lifelines, binding us together and pushing us forward. I vividly remember the times one of my siblings would take me by the hand, guiding me out of the room when tension rose, finding ways to distract me—whether through schoolwork, a game, or just being outdoors. They wanted to protect me from the harsh realities they themselves had to face.

As I grew older, I understood the depth of their sacrifices. The smiles and laughter they shared with me often masked the pain they endured. They bore the brunt of our father's anger so that I could experience a childhood free from fear, even if only in part. In shielding me, they shouldered the weight of our family's struggles, allowing me to hold on to hope. Now, I see God's hand in those moments. He placed them in my life as guardians, fulfilling a purpose neither they nor I could see then. Their quiet strength and unwavering love were a gift that sustained me—a reflection of Christ's call to bear each other's burdens. It wasn't loud or dramatic, but a constant, sacrificial love that shielded me from the worst.

As my siblings often wonder reflects from their stories, we wondered how different our lives might have been without their protection. The love of our mothers and the love, we have for each other even amidst our own suffering, kept us grounded. Looking back, we realize they were living out the words of Galatians *6:2: "Bear one another's burdens, and so fulfill the law of Christ."*

Through their love, we spared from the depths of despair that might have otherwise defined our childhood. Today, we are stronger, braver, and more compassionate because of them. We choose to live in hope, knowing that healing is possible, and that love can truly transform even the darkest of journeys.

Prayer for Gratitude for Family:

Dear Lord God,

Heavenly Father, thank You for the gift of my siblings and for the love and protection they provided when I needed it most. Help me to never take them for granted and to always remember the sacrifices they made for me. May I be a source of strength and love for them, just as they were for me. Guide me in showing them the same compassion and care they showed me.

And Lord, for all the burdens they carried in silence, I ask that You give them peace, healing, and the joy that only You can provide.

Chapter 4: My Siblings—My Silent Protectors

In Yeshua's name, Amen.

Five

Chapter 5: The Role of Faith in Our Family

Even though the chaos in our home often seemed overwhelming, one thing remained constant throughout my childhood—faith. Despite the arguments, the shouting, and the unpredictable tempers that filled our home, my mother made sure that we never drifted too far from God. It was as if, no matter how dark things became inside the walls of our house, there was always a flicker of light guiding us back to faith.

Sunday mornings were a sacred time in our household. My mother made sure that we went to church, no matter what had happened the night before. I can still picture her getting us ready, making sure we were dressed in our Sunday best, even if we had barely slept due to the turmoil in the home. For her, church was more than just a routine—it was a lifeline, a place where she could find the strength to keep going.

Sitting in the pews of that small church, I remember feeling an odd sense of calm, even if it was just for a few hours. The church was a stark contrast to the atmosphere at home. There was something comforting about the routine of the service, the familiar hymns, and the sound of people joining together in prayer. As a child, I didn't fully understand what faith meant, but I felt it in those moments. When we sang hymns, I remember the peace that would wash over me, even if it was fleeting. It was as if, for that brief period, I was able to breathe a little easier.

It was in that church where I began to sense the power of faith, even if I didn't have the words for it back then. The quiet reverence of the sanctuary provided a temporary escape from the storm at home. As we bowed our heads in prayer, I felt as though I was part of something bigger than myself. I didn't realize it at the time, but those small moments were sowing the seeds of faith that would later take root in my life.

My Mother's Anchor of Faith

Looking back, I now realize how much my mother's faith was the anchor that held us all together. While my father's anger and the instability of our home could have easily drowned us in despair.

My mother's unwavering belief in God kept us afloat. She didn't just attend church out of obligation—she prayed fervently, day in and day out. Whether she was cooking, cleaning, or sitting quietly at night, her lips were always moving in prayer. She carried the weight of our family's struggles on her shoulders, but she didn't do it alone. Her faith in God was her constant source of strength.

As a child, I didn't fully grasp the depth of her prayers, but

I could sense their importance. I would sometimes catch her kneeling beside her bed late at night, her hands clasped together, her head bowed. She would speak softly, almost whispering, pouring out her heart to God, asking for His guidance and protection. I didn't always understand what she was praying for, but I knew it was important. It was as if she was fighting a battle that none of us could see—a battle for our family's survival.

Now, as an adult, I understand that her prayers were not just for herself—they were for all of us. She prayed for our protection, for our safety, and for the strength to endure whatever came our way. She asked God to watch over us when she couldn't, to be our refuge when our home felt like a battlefield. Her faith sustained her, but it also sustained all of us, even if we didn't realize it at the time.

Church as a Refuge

Church wasn't just a place we went to on Sundays—it was our refuge. When the world around us seemed to be falling apart, church became the place where we could find peace. It was the one place where I knew we were safe. Inside those walls, I didn't have to worry about my father's temper or the chaos that often awaited us at home. For a few hours each week, we were free. We were part of a community that cared for us, prayed for us, and supported us.

It was in that small church where I first began to understand God's love and grace. The pastor would speak about God's unconditional love for His children, and I would wonder if that love extended to me. Could God really love me, even with all the pain and confusion in my life? I didn't know for sure back then, but the idea of God's love was like a beacon of hope. It was something to hold onto, even amid the darkness.

I also began to understand grace—not the kind of grace that we earn by being good enough, but the kind of grace that God offers freely to all of us, no matter what. I didn't fully grasp it at the time, but those early lessons in faith planted the seeds of hope in my heart. They gave me something to cling to, even when everything else felt uncertain.

Faith That Sustained Us Through the Storms

As I grew older, I began to see just how much our family's faith sustained us through the most difficult times. My mother's prayers, the support of our church, and the belief that God was with us—even when things were at their worst—gave us the strength to keep going. I now know that God was with us through it all, even when it didn't feel like it. He was with us in the chaos, in the pain, and in the moments when we felt like we couldn't take any more.

Those early lessons in faith have stayed with me throughout my life. They've shaped the way I see the world, the way I navigate hardship, and the way I understand God's presence in my life. Faith is not something that shields us from suffering—it's something that carries us through it. It's the belief that, even when everything seems to be falling apart, God is still with us. He is still in control.

I realize now that our faith was a lifeline. It was the thread that held us together when everything else was fraying at the edges. It didn't make the pain go away, but it gave us the strength to endure it. It didn't solve our problems, but it reminded us that we weren't facing them alone.

"The Lord is near to all who call on him, to all who call on him in truth." — **Psalm 145:18 (NIV)**

Prayer for Faith and Guidance

Dear Lord,

Thank You for the faith that sustained my family through the darkest times. Thank You for my mother's prayers and for the lessons I learned about Your love and grace. Help me to hold onto that faith, especially when I feel lost or afraid. Guide me, Lord, and lead me in Your truth.

Let me never forget that You are with me, even amid the storm. Strengthen my faith so that I may continue to trust in You, no matter what comes my way.

In Yeshua's name, Amen.

Six

Chapter 6: The Emotional Toll of Domestic Violence

Living in a home where domestic violence was a regular occurrence left scars on my heart and mind that I didn't fully understand until many years later. As a child, I had no frame of reference. I thought the volatility, the fear, the shouting, and the unpredictability were just a part of life, because it was all I knew. It was my normal. It never occurred to me that other families didn't live like this. It was just the way things were in our house.

I remember always feeling on edge, always waiting for something to go wrong. The tension in our home was palpable, like an unspoken weight hanging in the air. Sometimes, I felt like I couldn't breathe. I was constantly trying to read the room, gauge the mood, and figure out what I needed to do to keep the peace. It was exhausting. But it wasn't until I was older, when I began to see how other families lived, that I realized just how unhealthy and damaging that environment had been. It was only when I spent time with friends and their families that I began to understand how different their lives were. I would see them laugh together, relax around each other, and go through a day without the constant tension that had become so familiar to me. There were no raised voices, no angry silences, no walking on eggshells. I remember feeling confused, almost envious, as I watched them interact so freely and lovingly. It was like watching a scene from a movie that I couldn't be a part of.

Those early realizations were the first time I started to understand that my childhood wasn't normal—that the chaos and fear I had lived with were not what a home should feel like. And with that understanding came a flood of emotions that I wasn't prepared to deal with.

Carrying the Emotional Weight into Adulthood

The fear and confusion I experienced as a child followed me into adulthood like a shadow I couldn't escape. For years, I carried the emotional weight of those early experiences without even realizing it. It shaped how I saw the world, how I interacted with people, and most importantly, how I saw myself.

The anger I felt toward my father was deep and all-consuming at times. I wanted so badly to understand him, to figure out why he was the way he was, but all I could feel was resentment. How could he treat us like that? How could he let his temper, and his drinking destroy the family we could have been? I was angry at him for the pain he caused, but I was also angry at myself for still loving him despite everything.

Then there was the sadness I felt for my mother. She endured so much, and I often felt powerless to help her. She was a strong woman, but even the strongest people have limits. Seeing her weather the storms of our household took a toll on me. I could see the weariness in her eyes, the way she tried to protect us while also bearing the brunt of my father's temper. I admired her strength, but it broke my heart to see her suffer.

And then there was the uncertainty I felt about myself. Growing up in an environment where I was constantly on guard, constantly bracing for the next outburst, left me questioning my own worth. I wondered if I had done something to deserve the chaos around me. Was I part of the problem? Could I have done more to keep the peace? Those thoughts stayed with me for a long time, eating away at my sense of self-worth.

I didn't realize it at the time, but all those emotions—the anger, the sadness, the uncertainty—were slowly chipping away at me. They were like invisible wounds, hidden just beneath the surface, but they were there, shaping every decision I made and every relationship I entered. It wasn't until much later that I began to confront the truth: I had been deeply affected by the trauma of my childhood, and those emotional scars weren't going to heal on their own.

The Process of Healing

Healing from the trauma of domestic violence isn't something that happens overnight. It's a long, often painful process that requires confronting feelings you've spent years trying to bury. For a long time, I thought that if I just ignored the pain, it would eventually go away. But that's not how healing works. You can't outrun your past, and you can't numb the pain forever. Eventually, you must face it head-on.

For me, the first step in that process was acknowledging the pain. I had to stop pretending that I was okay. I had to admit to myself that my childhood had left deep emotional wounds, and that those wounds were affecting my life in ways I hadn't even realized. That acknowledgment was difficult—it felt like opening a door I had kept locked in years. But it was also necessary.

Once I opened that door, the emotions I had kept buried for so long came flooding back. The anger, the sadness, the confusion—it all hit me at once. I had to face the fact that the trauma I experienced as a child wasn't just something I could forget. It was part of me, and it was going to take time and effort to heal from it.

I sought help, talking to people I trusted and allowing myself to be vulnerable. For so long, I had been afraid to admit how much I was hurting. But as I started to open, I realized that healing didn't have to be something I did alone. God was with me, guiding me through the process, and so were the people who loved me.

"The Lord is close to the brokenhearted and saves those who are crushed in spirit." — Psalm 34:18 (NIV) This verse has been a source of comfort to me throughout my healing journey. It reminds me that God is always near, especially in the moments when my heart feels the heaviest. Even when the pain feels overwhelming, I know that I am not alone. God is with me, holding me close, and offering me the healing that only He can provide.

Prayer for Emotional Healing

Dear Lord, God

Lord, I come to You with a broken heart, asking for Your healing. I know that the emotional scars from my childhood have affected me deeply, and I need Your grace to heal. Help me to release the pain and trust in Your love and guidance.

Show me how to let go of the anger and sadness and replace it with Your peace. Heal the wounds that I carry, and restore my spirit, Lord.

Lead me on the path to wholeness and let me feel Your presence every step of the way.

In Yeshua's name, Amen.

Seven

Chapter 7: Finding Forgiveness for My Father

Forgiveness was one of the hardest things I had to grapple with when it came to my father. For years, I didn't even consider it. I carried the weight of anger and resentment like armor—believing that holding onto those feelings was my way of protecting myself from further hurt. In my mind, forgiving him felt like I was somehow letting him off the hook for all the chaos, fear, and emotional damage he caused. How could I possibly let go of those feelings when they had shaped so much of my life?

I blamed him for the instability in our home, for the moments of terror that still haunted me, for the confusion that lingered long after I became an adult. It wasn't just about the violent outbursts or the unpredictable rage; it was about all the quiet moments that were stolen from me, the laughter that should have filled our home, and the peace that was never there. It

34

was hard to imagine forgiving someone who had taken all that away.

I didn't realize at the time that the anger I held onto was hurting me far more than it was affecting him. I thought it was a form of self-preservation, a way to stay strong in the face of everything I had endured. But over time, I began to see that holding onto that anger was like drinking poison and expecting someone else to suffer. The bitterness was festering inside of me, affecting not just my relationship with my father but my relationship with myself and with others.

The decision to forgive didn't happen overnight. In fact, it was a process that took years of prayer, reflection, and deep emotional work. I had to confront the pain head-on, and that wasn't easy. I realized that I couldn't simply push the hurt aside and pretend it didn't exist. I had to acknowledge it, feel it, and understand where it was coming from. Forgiveness wasn't about excusing my father's behavior or pretending that everything was fine—it was about freeing myself from the burden of resentment.

One of the turning points in my journey toward forgiveness was understanding that forgiveness didn't mean reconciliation. It didn't mean that I had to have a close relationship with my father, or that I had to subject myself to the same patterns of behavior. Forgiveness was about releasing the grip that bitterness had on my heart. It was about choosing to let go of the pain that had defined me for so long, so that I could finally move forward.

Forgiveness is often misunderstood as a sign of weakness, but I came to realize that it takes incredible strength to forgive. It takes courage to face the hurt and choose to let it go. Holding onto anger might feel like power, but true strength comes from releasing the hold that anger has over you. It wasn't easy—there were many moments where I felt like giving up on the idea of forgiveness altogether. But with each prayer, with each step forward, I felt lighter. I was no longer carrying the weight of the past on my shoulders.

I also had to come to terms with the fact that forgiveness wasn't just about my father—it was about me. I couldn't move forward in my life, I couldn't find true peace, until I let go of the anger I had been carrying for so long. It was like dragging a heavy chain behind me, always there, always weighing me down. The only way to truly heal was to let that chain go.

Prayer and reflection

Through prayer and reflection, I began to see my father not just as the man who had caused me pain, but as someone who was deeply flawed and broken himself. That doesn't mean I excused his actions, but it gave me a different perspective. He had his own battles, his own wounds, and while that didn't justify what he did, it helped me understand that his behavior wasn't about me. His anger and drinking were his struggles, not a reflection of my worth.Forgiving him didn't mean I forgot the pain or that the memories of my childhood suddenly disappeared. But it did mean that I no longer let those memories control me.

I found freedom in forgiveness—not for my father's sake, but for my own. *"Be kind and compassionate to one another, forgiving each other, just as in Christ God forgave you."* — **Ephesians 4:32 (NIV)**

Prayer for Forgiveness

Dear Lord,

Lord, help me to forgive my father for the pain he caused. I know that holding onto anger only hurts me, and I ask for Your grace to let it go. Teach me to forgive, just as You have forgiven me. Help me to release the bitterness that has been weighing me down and guide me toward healing.

Fill my heart with compassion and peace, so that I can move forward in love and freedom.

In Yeshua's name, Amen.

Eight

Chapter 8: Learning to Love Through the Pain

Despite everything, I never stopped loving my father. I don't know how to fully explain that, but love is complicated. There were moments in my childhood, moments when my father was sober, when I could see the man, he was capable of being. He worked hard, he provided for us, and in those brief periods, he seemed to care deeply for our family. I saw glimpses of the man he could have been—the man I wished he could be all the time.

But loving him was never simple. It was always intertwined with pain, confusion, and anger. How do you love someone who causes so much hurt? That was the question I wrestled with for years. I wanted to love him—I wanted to be the kind of daughter who could look up to her father with admiration and pride. But every time I tried to embrace the good in him, the memories of the bad would rush back. It was like being torn between two conflicting emotions, never quite knowing how to reconcile them.

For a long time, I thought that loving someone meant excusing their behavior. I thought that if I loved my father, it meant that I had to forgive and forget the damage he had caused. But I've since learned that love is more complex than that. Love doesn't mean ignoring the pain—it means acknowledging it but choosing to love anyway. Love is a choice, not a feeling, and sometimes that choice is hard.

Loving my father meant coming to terms with the fact that he was a flawed and broken person. It meant understanding that his actions, while hurtful, reflected his own struggles, not a reflection of my worth. It took time, but I eventually realized that I could love my father without condoning his behavior. I could love him and still set boundaries. I could love him and still hold him accountable for the hurt he caused.

One of the most powerful lessons I've learned through this process is that love has the power to heal, even the deepest wounds. The love I had for my father didn't erase the pain, but it softened the edges of that pain. It allowed me to see him not just as the man who hurt me, but as someone who was struggling in ways I couldn't fully understand.

Loving through the pain doesn't mean letting go of boundaries. It doesn't mean allowing yourself to be hurt repeatedly. But it does mean choosing to see the humanity in the person who caused you pain. It means acknowledging that love, at its core, is about grace. And while it's not easy, love has a way of bringing healing where anger and bitterness cannot. *"**Above all, love each other deeply, because love covers over a multitude of sins.**" — 1 Peter 4:8 (NIV)*

Prayer for Healing Through Love

Dear Lord,

Help me to love through the pain. I know that love is not always easy, but I believe that it has the power to heal. Teach me how to love those who have hurt me, without excusing their actions. Let Your love be my guide and help me to find peace in the complexity of human relationships. Remind me that love, at its core, is about grace.

Let Your grace flow through me, bringing healing where bitterness once lived.

In Yeshua's name, Amen.

Nine

Chapter 9: The Role of Community in My Healing

Growing up, I never fully realized just how much the community we lived in helped me survive the emotional storms at home. At the time, the focus was on just getting through each day, but looking back now, I can clearly see the profound impact that the people around us had on my healing. Our neighbors, church members, and friends became an extended family—one that offered a kind of support that was missing in our home. In many ways, they were the foundation of stability in a world that often felt like it was crumbling

In our tight-knit community, everyone seemed to know everyone else's business, but instead of feeling invasive, it felt comforting. When things got bad at home, when my father's temper flared or the chaos felt overwhelming, there was always someone there—a neighbor who would check in, a friend's mother who would offer a warm meal, or a church member who would quietly pray for us. It was like having a safety net that caught me when I was falling, even when I didn't realize I needed to be caught.

I distinctly remember the warmth and love that radiated from our church. It wasn't just about attending Sunday services; it was about being part of something larger than myself. The church community was where I learned about compassion, grace, and unconditional support. The members of our congregation didn't just see us as the children of a man who struggled with anger and alcohol; they saw us as individuals who needed love and care. They would wrap their arms around us, quite literally at times, and make sure we knew we were loved.

Finding a place to escape

There were times when I would escape to a friend's house, seeking refuge from the tension at home. I'd sit at their dinner table, watching how their family interacted—how they laughed, how they shared stories, how they seemed so at ease with one another. It was in those moments that I realized what I was missing at home, but it was also in those moments that I felt a glimmer of hope. Their kindness and normalcy gave me something to hold onto. It reminded me that life didn't have to be defined by anger and fear.

As I've grown older, I've come to appreciate the role that community played in my healing. I realize now that I wasn't meant to carry the weight of my family's struggles on my own. The people around me—those neighbors, friends, and church members—helped carry that weight, even when I didn't know how to ask for help. Their quiet acts of kindness were like lifelines, pulling me out of the darkness and showing me that I didn't have to face my pain alone.

Community has the power to lift us up in ways we may not fully understand until we look back. It offers a sense of belonging, of being seen and valued, even when everything else feels uncertain. Healing, I've learned, is not something we do in isolation. It happens in the context of relationships—with the people who walk alongside us, hold our hands, and remind us that we are not alone. The love and care I received from my community played a critical role in my healing, even before I knew I needed healing.

As I continue my journey toward wholeness, I've learned to lean on my community more and more. I've realized that I don't have to be strong all the time, that it's okay to ask for help, and that there's power in allowing others to support me. Community is a gift, one that God places in our lives to help carry the burdens that feel too heavy to carry alone.

"Carry each other's burdens, and in this way, you will fulfill the law of Christ." — **Galatians 6:2 (NIV)**

Prayer for Community Support

Dear Lord, God,

Father, thank You for the gift of community. Thank You for placing people in my life who have supported me, encouraged me, and helped me carry my burdens when they felt too heavy. Help me to always appreciate and lean on the people You've placed around me. May I also be a source of strength, love, and support for others who need it.

Let me never forget the importance of community in healing and in fulfilling Your will.

In Yeshua's name Amen.

Ten

Chapter 10: Healing and Wholeness

Healing is not a straight path. I used to think that healing would come all at once, like a magical moment where everything would suddenly feel better. But what I've learned is that healing is more like a winding road, with its ups and downs, setbacks, and breakthroughs. It's a journey, and like any journey, it's filled with moments of triumph and moments of struggle. For me, the process of healing has been both painful and freeing, but every step has been necessary.

I spent years trying to suppress the pain of my childhood, thinking that if I ignored it long enough, it would go away. But pain has a way of resurfacing, often when we least expect it. I had to confront the trauma I experienced head-on, which meant revisiting some of the most difficult memories of my life. It meant sitting with the hurt, the anger, and the confusion, and allowing myself to feel it all. At times, the process felt overwhelming, like I was reopening wounds that had never properly healed.

But through that pain, I've come to realize that healing isn't about erasing the past. It's about finding wholeness in the present. It's about taking the pain and using it as fuel for growth. It's about acknowledging the scars, but not letting them define me. The scars are there—they will always be a part of my story—but they don't dictate who I am. Instead, they are a testament to how far I've come and to the strength I've gained along the way.

One of the most important lessons I've learned in my healing journey is that healing is not a destination—it's a lifelong process. There are still days when I feel the weight of the past pressing down on me, days when the old wounds feel fresh. But those days are fewer and farther between now. I've learned to give myself grace, to understand that healing doesn't mean being perfect. It means being whole, even with the broken pieces.

Cornerstone of My Healing

My faith has been the cornerstone of my healing. I've come to trust that God is leading me on this journey, even when I don't understand where it's going. He has been with me every step of the way, guiding me through the dark moments and celebrating with me in the moments of light. It's through my relationship with God that I've found true healing—healing that goes beyond the surface and touches the deepest parts of my soul.

I've also found healing in my relationships. The people in my life—my friends, family, and community—have been a source of strength and support. They've walked with me through the hard times, offering love, encouragement, and understanding. Through these relationships, I've learned that healing isn't something we do alone. We heal in connection with others, just as much as we heal in connection with ourselves and with God.

As I reflect on my journey toward healing and wholeness, I feel a sense of peace that I didn't have before. The pain of my childhood is still there, but it no longer holds the same power over me. I've learned to embrace the person I've become, scars and all. I'm still on this journey, and I know there will be challenges ahead, but I also know that I have the tools, the faith, and the support to continue healing.

"He heals the brokenhearted and binds up their wounds." — **Psalm 147:3 (NIV)**

Prayer for Healing and Wholeness

Dear Lord,

I thank You for the healing that has already taken place in my life, and I trust that You are continuing to lead me toward wholeness. I know that healing is a journey, and I ask for Your guidance every step of the way. Help me to continue to grow, to heal, and to use my experiences to become stronger.

Thank You for being with me in both the dark moments and the moments of light. I trust in Your plan for my life, and I ask for Your continued grace and love as I move forward.

In Yeshua's name, Amen.

Eleven

Chapter 11: Protection and Love

As much as my siblings and I endured during our childhood, my younger brother's experience was markedly different. Being the youngest of seven, he was six years younger than the rest of us, and by the time he came of age, much of the chaos in our household had simmered down. In some ways, it felt as though he had been spared from the worst of my father's abusive behavior. He grew up in the same house, with the same dysfunctional dynamics, but somehow, he was shielded in a way that I hadn't been.

I now realize that my mother, having already seen the toll my father's alcoholism and abuse had taken on us older children, went to great lengths to protect my brother from the worst of it. She couldn't change my father, but she could buffer the effects of his actions on my brother. And she did that with a fierce love and determination.

For my brother, this manifested in subtle yet profound ways.

Our mother would often keep him busy with tasks and activities, keeping him out of harm's way when she knew my father was on the verge of a violent episode. I remember her sending him off to play outside or take him to a relative's house for the weekend when things got particularly bad at home. She did whatever she could to maintain a sense of normalcy for him, even when the rest of us were suffering from the brunt of our father's outbursts.

My brother didn't grow up hearing the same arguments, seeing the same fights, or feeling the same terror that I had. Instead, he had the benefit of being in the company of a mother who was softer with him, knowing that this was her last chance to raise a child without the shadow of our father's abuse darkening every moment. She poured into him the love and protection that she couldn't always give to us in the same way. I think in many ways, my brother felt loved in a way that was foreign to the rest of us. While the love was always there for all of us, my mother had learned how to show it more openly by the time my brother came along. She wrapped him in her affection, shielding him from the reality we were all too familiar with. He was the baby of the family, and he knew it. The rest of us took on the role of his protectors as well, understanding that if anyone had a chance to escape the wounds we carried, it would be him. We didn't resent him for this, though; we were grateful that he had a different experience. It was almost as though his childhood represented what ours could have been if things had been different.

In conversations with my brother as we grew older, I realized that he felt this protection deeply. He understood, in his own way, that the family had taken great care to keep him safe—emotionally, physically, and mentally. He didn't have the same scars that the rest of us carried. But he also understood that this protection wasn't just happenstance; it was intentional, a result of our collective effort, and most importantly, the result of my mother's unwavering love.

My mother was a fortress for him, a shield that deflected the worst of the pain and trauma. Her protection allowed him to grow up in an environment where love, not fear, was his dominant experience. As I reflect on his story, I realize how profound a mother's love can be. Even when she couldn't change our father, she still found ways to give my brother the childhood that the rest of us didn't have. And in doing so, she showed all of us the power of protection, resilience, and love. *"The Lord is my strength and my shield; my heart trusts in Him, and He helps me. My heart leaps for joy, and with my song I praise Him."* — **Psalm 28:7 (NIV)**

Prayer for Mothers Who Protect

Dear Lord, God.

Heavenly Father, thank You for the strength and love of mothers who protect their children, even in the most difficult circumstances. I lift my mother, who shielded my brother from the worst of our family's pain. Thank You for giving her the wisdom and courage to protect him, and for the love she showed all of us.

I ask that You continue to guide and bless mothers everywhere who are doing their best to protect their children from harm.

Help them to feel Your presence and strength.

Chapter 11: Protection and Love

In Yeshua's name Amen.

Twelve

Chapter 12: Reconciliation with Myself

One of the hardest parts of my healing journey has been reconciling with myself. The years I spent growing up in an abusive environment left deep scars on my soul, and for the longest time, I carried a heavy weight of guilt, shame, and confusion. I felt like I was complicit in the chaos simply because I was there. I blamed myself for not doing more to stop the abuse, for not speaking up when things went wrong. The questions played over and over in my mind, "Why didn't I try harder to stop it? Could I have prevented it somehow?"

As I grew older, this guilt didn't dissipate—it only grew stronger. I started seeing myself as unworthy of love and forgiveness because I couldn't save my family from the pain. This distorted self-image weighed me down for years, as I carried the burdens of my past like a chain around my heart. But as I began to walk on the path toward healing, I came to a powerful and life-changing realization: the reconciliation I truly needed wasn't just with my father or the circumstances surrounding my childhood—it was with myself. I had to forgive myself for the things I couldn't control, for the role I thought I should have played as a child but couldn't.

God began to work on my heart, showing me that healing starts with grace—grace toward others, yes, but also grace toward myself. For so long, I was my own worst critic, replaying the events of my childhood and thinking of all the ways I could have "done better." I held myself responsible for the things I couldn't have changed, for actions and reactions that were far beyond my control. It took years for me to realize that none of this was my fault. The abuse, the violence—it wasn't mine to own. I had to release the burden of blame and stop condemning myself for the past.

It wasn't an easy truth to accept. Self-forgiveness is often the most difficult kind of forgiveness. For so long, I believed that I wasn't worthy of love or redemption. But God, in His infinite mercy, showed me that His love isn't based on my perfection or my actions—His love is unconditional, rooted in His grace. I came to understand that God doesn't love us because we are flawless; He loves us simply because we are His children. In the same way, I've learned to love myself—not in a perfect way, but in the way that acknowledges my humanity, my brokenness, and my ongoing journey toward wholeness.

The process of reconciling with myself required me to silence the voices in my head that said I was "less than" or "unworthy." Those voices had been there for so long that I had come to accept them as part of my identity. But God's voice speaks louder. He says I am worthy. He says I am loved. And through His grace, I have learned to see myself as He sees me—imperfect, but whole; flawed, but loved.

Forgive Yourself

I had to forgive myself for carrying shame that was never mine to bear. I had to let go of the anger I directed toward myself, and instead, embrace the love and compassion that God pours out on me daily. It was in this surrender that I found the beginnings of true healing. Reconciliation with oneself is a slow process, and it doesn't happen overnight. There are days when I still struggle to see myself through the eyes of grace. But each day, I remind myself that God's love for me is greater than my self-condemnation. He sees me, He knows my pain, and He calls me beloved. The more I lean into His love, the more I can reconcile with the person in the mirror—the person I've judged so harshly for so long.

I've learned that healing is not about erasing the past or pretending the pain didn't happen. Instead, it's about accepting that the past is part of my story, but it doesn't define who I am today. I am no longer bound by the guilt and shame of my childhood. Instead, I walk in the freedom that comes from self-acceptance, from reconciliation with myself, and from the deep understanding that I am a child of God. ***For if our heart condemns us, God is greater than our heart and knows all things."*** — **1 John 3:20 (NKJV)**

Prayer for Self-Reconciliation

Dear Lord,

Lord, I come before You with a heart that has been hard on itself for far too long. I ask for Your help in reconciling with myself and letting go of the shame and guilt I have carried. Help me to forgive myself for the things I couldn't control and the burdens I wasn't meant to bear.

Replace the lies I have believed with Your truth—that I am worthy, loved, and redeemed in Your eyes.

Teach me to see myself as You see me and to walk in the freedom of Your grace.

In Yeshua's name Amen.

Thirteen

Chapter 13: Walking in Forgiveness and Love

Forgiving my father was one of the most difficult and painful journeys I've ever undertaken. The anger, resentment, and bitterness I held toward him were like chains around my heart, binding me to the darkest parts of my past. For years, I believed that holding onto that anger would protect me, that it would somehow prevent me from being hurt again. But over time, I realized that it wasn't protecting me—it was imprisoning me. It wasn't until I began to understand the true nature of forgiveness that I realized it was the key to my healing and freedom.

Forgiveness is a word that sounds simple in theory, but in practice, it's incredibly complex. It took me a long time to understand that forgiving my father wasn't about letting him off the hook for the pain he caused me. It wasn't about pretending that the abuse and hurt never happened. Forgiveness, I learned, wasn't about him at all—it was about me. It was about my healing, my freedom, and my ability to move forward.

Control Over the Pain

For years, I thought that holding onto my anger would some-how give me control over the pain I experienced. I thought that if I stayed angry, I could shield myself from ever being vulnerable again. But that anger only deepened my wounds. It kept me stuck in a cycle of hurt, replaying the painful memories over and over in my mind. I was still allowing my father's actions to control me long after the abuse had ended.

When I finally decided to forgive, I knew it would be a long process. It wasn't something that could happen overnight, and it certainly wasn't something I could do on my own. I had to pray—constantly. I had to ask God for the strength to release the bitterness I had been clinging to. And little by little, as I opened my heart to God's grace, I began to feel the chains of resentment start to loosen.

In those moments of prayer, God began to reveal something to me that changed the way I viewed forgiveness. He showed me that forgiveness is an act of love—not just for the person who hurt you, but for yourself. By holding onto anger and bitterness, I was allowing the pain of the past to continue to wound me. But by choosing to forgive, I was choosing to love myself enough to release the burden of that anger. I was choosing healing over hurt.

Forgiveness didn't mean that I condoned my father's behavior or that I pretended the abuse never happened. It didn't mean that I forgot the pain or the trauma. Instead, forgiveness meant that I was no longer going to allow the actions of my father to define me. It meant that I was choosing to release the emotional hold that the past had on me so that I could walk in freedom and healing.

As I continued to pray and ask God for guidance, I began to understand that forgiveness reflects God's love. Just as Christ forgave me, I am called to forgive others. It's not an easy call, but it is one of the most powerful acts of love we can offer—both to those who have hurt us and to ourselves.

Forgiveness is healing

Through forgiveness, I learned how to love again. I learned how to love not just my father, but also myself. In forgiving my father, I was able to release the toxic emotions that had kept me in bondage for so long. I was able to stop replaying the scenes of abuse in my mind and start focusing on my healing. I was able to love myself enough to stop living in the shadows of my past and step into the light of God's love and grace.

Forgiving my father didn't mean that I suddenly became immune to the pain of my childhood. There are still days when memories resurface, and I must remind myself of the healing that has taken place. But I now understand that forgiveness is a choice I must make every day. It's a decision to release the bitterness that tries to creep back into my heart and to walk in the love and grace of God.

Forgiveness has allowed me to reclaim my life. It has allowed me to move forward without the weight of anger dragging me down. Most importantly, it has allowed me to experience the fullness of God's love. The same love that gave me the strength to forgive my father is the love that continues to guide me as I walk this path of healing. *Be kind and compassionate to one another, forgiving each other, just as in Christ God forgave you.* — **Ephesians 4:32 (NIV)**

Prayer for Forgiveness

Dear Heavenly Father,

Father, I come to You with a heart that has been burdened by anger and bitterness. I ask for Your strength to forgive those who have hurt me, especially my father. I know that forgiveness reflects Your love, and I trust that You will help me release the bitterness that has held me captive for so long. Teach me to walk in love, even toward those who have caused me pain. Help me to see the healing power of forgiveness and to find peace in my heart.

I trust in Your grace to lead me toward freedom and wholeness.

In Yeshua's name, Amen.

Fourteen

Chapter 14: Rebuilding My Identity in Christ

The journey toward healing from domestic violence didn't end with forgiveness. In fact, forgiveness was just the beginning. After I let go of the bitterness and anger that had been weighing me down for so long, I was left with an emptiness I didn't know how to fill. For years, my identity had been shaped by the trauma I endured. I had allowed the abuse, the pain, and the hurt to define who I was. Once I forgave, I realized that I needed to rebuild—rebuild my heart, my mind, and my sense of self. I needed to rediscover who I was, not as a victim, but as a child of God.

For so long, I had seen myself through the lens of pain. I believed the lies that domestic abuse had planted in my mind: that I was unworthy, that I was broken, that I didn't deserve love or happiness. I carried these beliefs with me for years, and they influenced the way I saw myself and the way I related to others. But once I decided to forgive, I realized that I had to let go of those lies. I had to rebuild my identity based on who God says I am, not on what the world—or my abuser—tried to make me believe.

The process of rebuilding my identity in Christ has been one of the most challenging yet rewarding journeys I've ever experienced. It required me to look deep within myself and confront the insecurities and doubts that had taken root during my years of abuse. It meant learning to silence the voices in my head that told me I wasn't good enough, that I wasn't lovable, or that I wasn't worthy of healing. And instead, I had to tune into God's voice, the voice that reminded me of my worth, my value, and my identity as His beloved child.

I remember the first time I really began to understand what it meant to find my identity in Christ. I was reading through the Bible, and I came across a verse that changed everything for me: ***For we are God's handiwork, created in Christ Jesus to do good works, which God prepared in advance for us to do.*— Ephesians 2:10 (NIV)** The word "handiwork" struck me deeply. It made me realize that I wasn't just a broken person defined by my past; I was God's handiwork. He had created me with a purpose, and He saw value in me. I wasn't a mistake. I wasn't unworthy. I was designed by the Creator of the universe, and that gave me more worth than I had ever imagined.

The idea that God had prepared good works for me to do, even before I was born, was overwhelming. For so long, I believed that my life had no direction or purpose. But now I saw that God had a plan for me all along, even though the pain, even though the abuse. He had been preparing me for something greater, and my identity wasn't rooted in what had been done to me, but in what God had called me to be.

Rebuilding my identity in Christ wasn't an overnight process. It took—and still takes—intentionality. I had to be diligent about spending time in God's Word, allowing Him to remind me daily of who I am in Him. I had to replace the lies I had believed about myself with God's truth. It wasn't always easy. There were days when the old feelings of unworthiness would try to creep back in. But each time, I would turn to Scripture, and I would remind myself of God's promises. I began to meditate on verses like: *"I praise you because I am fearfully and wonderfully made; your works are wonderful; I know that full well."* — **Psalm 139:14 (NIV)**

God Is My Anchor

This verse became an anchor for me. It reminded me that I was created by God, and that I was wonderfully made. No matter what had happened to me in the past, no matter what anyone else had said or done, I was God's creation, and I was valuable in His eyes. Every time doubt tried to sneak back in, I clung to this verse, allowing it to reshape the way I saw myself. Another powerful verse that helped me on this journey was: **Therefore, if anyone is in Christ, the new creation has come: The old has gone, the new is here! — 2 Corinthians 5:17 (NIV)**

This verse reminded me that in Christ, I was a new creation. I didn't have to carry the baggage of my past with me. The old me, the one who had been hurt, abused, and broken, was gone. In Christ, I had been made new. My past no longer defined me—Christ did. This realization gave me a sense of freedom and hope that I had never known before. I was free from the chains of my past, and I could now walk in the fullness of the identity that Christ had given me.

Rebuilding my identity also meant surrounding myself with people who reminded me of God's truth. I had to be intentional about cultivating relationships with those who uplifted and encouraged me, those who saw me through the lens of Christ's love. My church community became a safe place where I could grow and heal. They didn't see me as broken—they saw me as redeemed.

One of the most beautiful things about rebuilding my identity in Christ was that it allowed me to love myself again. For so long, I had felt unlovable. But through this journey, I learned that God's love for me was unwavering, and if He loved me, then I could love myself too. This love wasn't based on perfection or performance—it was because I was His child, created in His image.

Learning to love myself also meant learning to care for myself. I began to prioritize my mental, emotional, and spiritual well-being. I allowed myself the grace to rest, to heal, and to grow. I sought counseling, not as a sign of weakness, but as an act of self-love, knowing that God desired wholeness for me in every area of my life.

As I reflect on this journey, I realize that the process of rebuilding my identity is ongoing. Every day, I choose to walk in the truth of who God says I am. Every day, I choose to reject the lies of the enemy and embrace the identity that Christ has given me. And every day, I thank God for the healing, freedom, and love that come from knowing who I am in Him. ***Therefore, if anyone is in Christ, the new creation has come: The old has gone, the new is here!"*** — **2 Corinthians 5:17 (NIV)**

Prayer for Rebuilding Identity

Dear Lord, God.

Lord, I thank You for the truth of who I am in You. I ask for Your help in continuing to rebuild my identity, not based on the lies of the past, but on the truth of Your Word. Help me to see myself as You see me—worthy, loved, and redeemed. Guide me as I walk in the fullness of who You've called me to be.

Let Your truth be my foundation, and let Your love be the lens through which I view myself.

In Yeshua's name, Amen.

Fifteen

Chapter 15: Freedom and Hope

After the long and painful journey of healing from domestic violence, forgiving my father, and rebuilding my identity in Christ, I realized that there was still one more step I had to take—embracing my future. For so long, my life had been defined by the trauma of my past, and even after I had forgiven, healed, and found a new sense of self, I struggled to look ahead with hope. It was as though I had learned how to survive, but I hadn't yet learned how to live freely. Chapter 15 is about that transition—about moving from survival to freedom and hope.

For years, I had lived in the shadow of my past, always looking over my shoulder, wondering if the pain would come back, if the nightmares would return. I had grown so accustomed to living in fear and doubt that even as I healed, I wasn't sure how to step into a future filled with hope. But as I continued to grow in my faith and lean on God's promises, I began to understand that He wasn't just healing my past—He was also preparing me for a future that was full of promise, joy, and freedom.

The process of embracing that future started with trust. I had to learn how to trust God not only with my healing but also with my future. It wasn't easy at first. I had spent so much of my life trying to control things, trying to protect myself from more hurt. But God was calling me to release that control and trust Him fully. I had to believe that He had good plans for me, plans that were beyond what I could imagine. This was a difficult transition because it meant letting go of my fears and fully surrendering to God's will.

There were days when I still felt doubt creeping in. I'd wonder if I was free or if the pain of my past would come back to haunt me. But each time those thoughts arose, I reminded myself of God's promises:

For I know the plans I have for you," declares the Lord, "plans to prosper you and not to harm you, plans to give you hope and a future." — **Jeremiah 29:11 (NIV)**

Trust God With My Future

This verse became a lifeline for me as I began to embrace the future. It reminded me that God's plans for my life were good, that He had not brought me this far to abandon me, and that the same God who healed me from the past would guide me into a future full of hope.

As I continued to trust God with my future, I started to dream again. For so long, my dreams had been buried under the weight of my pain. I had stopped dreaming about the kind of life I wanted to live, the things I wanted to accomplish, and the person I wanted to become. But as I embraced freedom in Christ, I realized that God was inviting me to dream again—to envision a future that was full of life, love, and purpose. It was as though He was saying, "Now that you are free, what will you do with that freedom?"

I began to write down my dreams, both big and small. I dreamed of living a life that glorified God in every way, of using my story to help others who had been through similar pain, and of walking in the fullness of the calling that God had placed on my life. These dreams weren't just wishes—they were rooted in the belief that God had a purpose for my life, and that He would equip me to fulfill that purpose.

As I moved forward in my healing, I also realized that part of embracing my future meant letting go of the "victim" mindset. For so long, I had identified myself as a victim of domestic violence, and while that was a part of my story, it wasn't the whole story. God had given me victory over my past, and He had called me to walk in that victory. Embracing my future meant stepping into the role of a victor, not a victim. It meant acknowledging that while the past had shaped me, it did not define me. My identity was in Christ, and in Him, I was more than a conqueror. **"No, in all these things we are more than conquerors through him who loved us." — Romans 8:37 (NIV)**

This verse reminded me that through Christ, I was victorious over the pain and trauma of my past. I didn't have to live in fear or doubt anymore. I was free to embrace a future that was full of hope, knowing that nothing could separate me from God's love. As I began to walk in that freedom, I also realized that my journey wasn't just about me. God had placed people in my life who needed to hear my story, people who were struggling with their own pain and trauma. I began to share my testimony with others, not as a way of dwelling on the past, but as a way of pointing them to the healing power of Christ. I wanted others to know that freedom was possible, that they didn't have to stay stuck in the cycle of pain and fear. God had set me free, and I wanted to help others find that same freedom.

God Was Using My Pain

Through sharing my story, I discovered a new sense of purpose. I realized that God was using my pain for His glory, that He was turning what the enemy meant for harm into something good. My life wasn't just about surviving—it was about thriving, about living out the calling that God had placed on my life, and about helping others do the same.

I also began to embrace joy in a way that I hadn't before. For so long, I had equated joy with the absence of pain, but now I understood that joy could coexist with healing. As I walked in freedom, I found joy in the little things—the laughter of my children, the beauty of nature, the love of my church community. Joy wasn't about perfection or the absence of struggle—it was about knowing that God was with me, that He had redeemed my story, and that He had a good future in store for me.

In embracing my future, I also had to learn to be patient. Healing is a lifelong process, and while I had come a long way, I knew there would still be challenges ahead. But I trusted that God would be with me every step of the way. I didn't have to have all the answers or know exactly what the future held I just had to trust that God did. And that was enough.

Being confident of this, that he who began a good work in you will carry it on to completion until the day of Christ Jesus." — **Philippians 1:6 (NIV)** This verse gave me the confidence to keep moving forward, knowing that the work God had begun in me wasn't finished yet. He was still at work in my life, and He would carry me through whatever challenges lay ahead. In Chapter 15, I reflect on the importance of embracing a future that is filled with freedom, hope, and purpose. It's about walking in the victory that Christ has already won for us and trusting that His plans for our lives are good. It's about dreaming again, finding joy in the present, and sharing our story to help others find healing. Most importantly, it's about trusting God with our future, knowing that He will carry us through whatever comes next.

For I know the plans I have for you," declares the Lord, "plans to prosper you and not to harm you, plans to give you hope and a future." — **Jeremiah 29:11 (NIV)**

Prayer for Embracing the Future

Dear Lord God,

Lord, I thank You for the healing and freedom You've brought into my life. As I look to the future, I ask for Your guidance and strength. Help me to trust in Your plans, to walk in the freedom You've given me, and to embrace the future with hope and joy. Teach me to dream again, to live boldly in Your love, and to share my story with others.

I know that You have good things in store for me, and I trust that You will carry me through whatever lies ahead.

In Yeshua's name, Amen.

II

Part II

A Journey of Healing, Faith, and Forgiveness

Sixteen

Day 01: A Prayer for Strength

Scripture: "**God is our refuge and strength, an ever-present help in trouble.**" **— Psalm 46:1 (NIV)**

Dear Heavenly Father,

I come to You today with a heart that feels weak and burdened by the weight of my experiences. I ask for Your strength to carry me through the pain of abuse and to remind me that You are always with me, even in the darkest moments. Help me to find comfort in Your presence and to know that I am never alone.

Give me the courage to seek help when I need it and the faith to trust that You will provide a way out.

In Yeshua's name, Amen.

Seventeen

Day 02: Prayer for Survival

Scripture: "Even though I walk through the darkest valley, I will fear no evil, for you are with me; your rod and your staff, they comfort me." — Psalm 23:4 (NIV)

Dear Lord, God,

Lord, as I walk through the valleys of fear and confusion, I ask that You guide me with Your love and comfort. Help me find moments of joy even during the darkness and to trust that You will lead me out of these shadows. Help me to survive, not by my strength alone, but by Yours.

Teach me to find joy in You, even when everything around me feels hopeless.

In Yeshua's name, Amen.

Eighteen

Day 03: Prayer for Protection

Scripture: "**Bear one another's burdens, and so fulfill the law of Christ.**" — **Galatians 6:2 (NIV)**

Dear Father,

I thank You for the protection and love my family has shown me throughout my life. Thank You for my siblings, who shielded me from harm when I was too young to protect myself. Bless them for their sacrifices and help me to carry their burdens as they carried mine.

May our family remain strong in Your love and continue to support one another through the trials of life.

In Yeshua's name Amen.

Nineteen

Day 04: A Prayer for Reconciliation with My Father

Scripture: **"Be kind and compassionate to one another, forgiving each other, just as in Christ God forgave you." — Ephesians 4:32 (NIV)**

Dear Lord,

Today, I bring before You the pain and anger I have held toward my father. I know that forgiveness is not easy, but I ask for Your help in letting go of the bitterness that has weighed on my heart. Teach me to forgive, not because his actions were right, but because You call me to walk in love and grace.

Help me to release the chains of resentment and to find peace in You.

Day 04: A Prayer for Reconciliation with My Father

In Yeshua's name, Amen.

Twenty

Day 05: A Prayer for Healing

❧❦❧

Scripture: "The Lord is close to the brokenhearted and saves those who are crushed in spirit." — Psalm 34:18 (NIV)

Dear Father,

I come to You today with a heart that is still broken from the scars of my past. I ask for Your healing touch upon my emotions, my mind, and my spirit. Help me to release the pain I have carried for so long and to trust that You will bind up my wounds.

Heal me from the inside out and restore my heart to wholeness.

In Yeshua's name, Amen.

Twenty-One

Day 06: A Prayer to Forgive Myself

Scripture: "For if our heart condemns us, God is greater than our heart and knows all things." — 1 John 3:20 (NKJV)

Dear Lord,

I often struggle with guilt and shame for the things I couldn't control as a child. Today, I ask for Your help in forgiving myself. Help me to see myself as You see me, washed clean by Your grace and love.

Remind me that I am not defined by my past, but by who You say I am—worthy, beloved, and forgiven.

In Yeshua's name Amen.

Twenty-Two

Day 07: A Prayer for Walking in Forgiveness

Scripture: "Be kind and compassionate to one another, forgiving each other, just as in Christ God forgave you." — Ephesians 4:32 (NIV)

Dear Father,

I choose today to walk in forgiveness. I know that this journey is not easy, but I trust that You are with me every step of the way. Help me to forgive those who have hurt me, not for their sake, but for mine. Free my heart from the bitterness and anger that has held me captive for so long.

Let Your love fills the spaces where resentment once lived and guide me toward a future of healing.

Day 07: A Prayer for Walking in Forgiveness

In Yeshua's name, Amen.

Twenty-Three

Day 08: A Prayer for Community and Support

Scripture: "Carry each other's burdens, and in this way, you will fulfill the law of Christ." — Galatians 6:2 (NIV)

Dear Lord,

Lord, I thank You for the community You have placed around me. Thank You for the people who have supported me, prayed for me, and carried my burdens when I couldn't carry them alone. Help me to lean on this community and to offer the same love and support to those in need.

Remind me that we are never meant to walk this journey alone.

In Yeshua's name, Amen.

Twenty-Four

Day 09: A Prayer for Embracing My Future

Scripture: "**For I know the plans I have for you,**" **declares the Lord, "plans to prosper you and not to harm you, plans to give you hope and a future.— Jeremiah 29:11 (NIV)**

Dear Father,

I thank You for the future You have planned for me. I ask for the courage to embrace that future with hope, joy, and trust. Help me to let go of the fears that have held me back and to walk boldly into the life You have prepared for me.

Guide my steps and give me the wisdom to follow Your will in every decision I make.

In Yeshua's name, Amen.

Twenty-Five

Day 10: A Prayer for Letting Go of the Past

Scripture: "No, in all these things we are more than conquerors through him who loved us." — Romans 8:37 (NIV)

Dear Lord,

I know that I have been more than a conqueror through Your love, yet there are days when I still feel the weight of my past. Help me to let go of the pain, shame, and hurt that no longer serve me.

Teach me to walk in the victory You have already won for me, knowing that I am free from the chains of my past.

In Yeshua's name, Amen.

Twenty-Six

Day 11: A Prayer for Healing

Scripture: **"He heals the brokenhearted and binds up their wounds." — Psalm 147:3 (NIV)**

Dear Father,

Father, you know the broken places in my heart better than I do. I ask for Your healing touch today. Heal the wounds that still ache, the parts of me that still feel broken. Bind up my heart with Your love and restore me to wholeness.

Help me to trust in Your healing power and to believe that You are working all things for my good.

In Yeshua's name, Amen.

Twenty-Seven

Day 12: A Prayer for Reclaiming My Worth

∾⊱⊰∽

Scripture: "I praise you because I am fearfully and wonderfully made; your works are wonderful; I know that full well." — **Psalm 139:14 (NIV)**

Dear Lord,

God reminds me today that I am fearfully and wonderfully made. Help me to reclaim the worth that You have given me, the worth that no one can take away. Let Your truth speak louder than the lies I've believed about myself.

Help me to see myself through Your eyes—worthy, precious, and beloved. *In Yeshua's name* Amen.

Twenty-Eight

Day 13: A Prayer for Trusting God's Plans

Scripture: "Being confident of this, that he who began a good work in you will carry it on to completion until the day of Christ Jesus." — **Philippians 1:6 (NIV)**

Dear Father,

I thank You for the work You have started in my life. Help me to trust that You will carry it to completion. Even when I don't see the full picture, I know that You are at work. Give me patience and faith to trust in Your timing and Your plans for my life.

I believe that what You have started, you will finish.

In Yeshua's name, Amen.

Twenty-Nine

Day 14: A Prayer for Walking in Love

Scripture: "Above all, love each other deeply, because love covers over a multitude of sins." — 1 Peter 4:8 (NIV)

Dear Lord,

Lord, help me to walk in love every day, even when it's hard. Teach me to love those who have hurt me, to love myself, and to love those who need to know Your grace.

Let Your love flow through me, covering over the wounds of my past and bringing healing to my heart.

In Yeshua's name, Amen.

Thirty

Study Verses

Here are all the verses used from Chapter 1 through Chapter 16:

Chapter 1: Seeking Help in Pain

- **Matthew 19:26 (NIV)**: "With man this is impossible, but with God all things are possible."
- **Psalm 46:1 (NIV)**: "God is our refuge and strength, an ever-present help in trouble."

Chapter 2: Surviving the Present

- **Psalm 23:4 (NIV)**: "Even though I walk through the darkest valley, I will fear no evil, for you are with me; your rod and your staff, they comfort me."
- **Isaiah 43:4 (NIV)**: "You are precious and honored in my

sight, and because I love you, I will give people in exchange for you, nations in exchange for your life."

- **Psalm 46:10 (NIV)**: "Be still and know that I am God; I will be exalted among the nations, I will be exalted in the earth."
- **Philippians 4:13 (NKJV)**: "I can do all things through Christ who strengthens me."

Chapter 3: The Confusing Duality of My Father

- **Colossians 3:21 (NIV)**: "Fathers, do not embitter your children, or they will become discouraged."

Chapter 4: My Siblings—My Silent Protectors

- **Galatians 6:2 (NIV)**: "Bear one another's burdens, and so fulfill the law of Christ."

Chapter 5: The Role of Faith in Our Family

- **Psalm 145:18 (NIV)**: "The Lord is near to all who call on him, to all who call on him in truth."

Chapter 6: The Emotional Toll of Domestic Violence

- **Psalm 34:18 (NIV)**: "The Lord is close to the brokenhearted and saves those who are crushed in spirit."

Chapter 7: Finding Forgiveness for My Father

- **Ephesians 4:32 (NIV)**: "Be kind and compassionate to one another, forgiving each other, just as in Christ God forgave you."

Chapter 8: Learning to Love Through the Pain

- **1 Peter 4:8 (NIV)**: "Above all, love each other deeply, because love covers over a multitude of sins."

Chapter 9: The Role of Community in My Healing

- **Galatians 6:2 (NIV)**: "Carry each other's burdens, and in this way, you will fulfill the law of Christ."

Chapter 10: My Journey Toward Healing and Wholeness

- **Psalm 147:3 (NIV)**: "He heals the brokenhearted and binds up their wounds."

Chapter 11: Protection and Love from My Mother

- **Proverbs 31:28 (NIV)**: "Her children arise and call her blessed; her husband also, and he praises her."

Chapter 12: Reconciliation with Myself

- **1 John 3:20 (NKJV)**: "For if our heart condemns us, God is greater than our heart and knows all things."

Chapter 13: Walking in Forgiveness and Love

- **Ephesians 4:32 (NIV)**: "Be kind and compassionate to one another, forgiving each other, just as in Christ God forgave you."

Chapter 14: Finding Closure and Releasing Guilt

- **Isaiah 61:3 (NIV)**: "To provide for those who grieve in Zion— to bestow on them a crown of beauty instead of ashes, the oil of joy instead of mourning, and a garment of praise instead of a spirit of despair."

Chapter 15: Embracing God's Purpose for My Life

- **Jeremiah 29:11 (NIV)**: "For I know the plans I have for you," declares the Lord, "plans to prosper you and not to harm you, plans to give you hope and a future."

Chapter 16: Daily Prayers for Healing, Freedom, and Hope

- **Psalm 46:1 (NIV)**: "God is our refuge and strength, an ever-present help in trouble."
- **Psalm 23:4 (NIV)**: "Even though I walk through the darkest valley, I will fear no evil, for you are with me; your rod and your staff, they comfort me."
- **Galatians 6:2 (NIV)**: "Bear one another's burdens, and so fulfill the law of Christ."
- **Ephesians 4:32 (NIV)**: "Be kind and compassionate to one another, forgiving each other, just as in Christ God forgave you."
- **Psalm 34:18 (NIV)**: "The Lord is close to the brokenhearted and saves those who are crushed in spirit."
- **1 John 3:20 (NKJV)**: "For if our heart condemns us, God is greater than our heart and knows all things."

- **Jeremiah 29:11 (NIV)**: "For I know the plans I have for you," declares the Lord, "plans to prosper you and not to harm you, plans to give you hope and a future."
- **Romans 8:37 (NIV)**: "No, in all these things we are more than conquerors through him who loved us."
- **Psalm 147:3 (NIV)**: "He heals the brokenhearted and binds up their wounds."
- **Psalm 139:14 (NIV)**: "I praise you because I am fearfully and wonderfully made; your works are wonderful; I know that full well."
- **Philippians 1:6 (NIV)**: "Being confident of this, that he who began a good work in you will carry it on to completion until the day of Christ Jesus."
- **1 Peter 4:8 (NIV)**: "Above all, love each other deeply, because love covers over a multitude of sins."

These verses have guided the prayers and reflections throughout the journey of healing, forgiveness, and finding strength in God. Each verse speaks to a different aspect of that process, offering biblical wisdom and comfort.

Afterword

⁕⁕⁕

"Abuse is a heavy burden, and no one should have to bear it alone."

I met Mary years ago at Agape Fellowship Ministries, and we've been kindred spirits ever since. She is a light in my life and vital to my village. This book reflects the truths Mary constantly reminds me of: I am an overcomer, fearfully and wonderfully made, and a child of the Most High God. Through her testimony, Mary has become an anointed vessel, helping those who have faced similar challenges. Her story reveals that even in the pain of abuse, there is purpose.

This book opens the conversation about healing, breaking the silence of shame, and guiding readers toward restoration. Dive into Mary's journey, feel the depth of her experiences, seek help, pray, and know that God sees you.

You are not alone. Mary's powerful intercession stems

from her mother's legacy, whose example ignited the fire we see today. Thank God for this spiritual journey and the healing it inspires.

I pray you embrace the truth within this book. The enemy often makes us feel isolated and ashamed of our struggles, but you are not alone.

Respectfully,

Leslie

Letter to the Reader

My Dearest Reader,

In the quiet moments, when the weight of the past seems to press down on your spirit, I want you to remember this: You are not defined by your scars, but by the courage that brought you through the fire.

There were days when the darkness seemed endless, when the hurt tried to convince you that you were broken beyond repair. Yet here you stand, triumphant and unyielding. Not because the pain wasn't real, but because your resilience was greater. You faced the storm, and instead of being swept away, you became a beacon of light for others to follow.

What a miracle it is to see your heart soft yet strong, willing to love and dream once again. Those dreams, once buried beneath the ashes of hurt, are now rising, filled with a new life—a life touched by God's grace, sculpted by His hands, and purposed for something far greater than you can imagine.

You have trusted God with your future, and in doing so, you have found the freedom to dream, to hope, to walk boldly into what lies ahead. No longer defined by the battles you've fought, you are stepping into the fullness of who you were always meant to be—strong, victorious, and cherished beyond measure.

I want you to know that you are loved with a love that transcends all understanding, a love that healed your wounds and replaced them with purpose. This love, dear one, will never leave you. It is the same love that carried you through the darkest valleys and now beckons you toward a future of abundant peace, joy, and fulfillment.

Embrace this truth: You are not a victim; you are a victor. In Christ, you have overcome. The chains of the past no longer bind you, and now you are free to dance in the light of all that God has prepared for you.So dream big, love boldly, and never forget—you are more than a conqueror. Your future is bright, and your story is a testimony of God's unfailing love and power to redeem.

With all my heart,

A Fellow Traveler on the Journey

Give
THANKS
to the Lord
for He is good; His love endures forever.
—1 Chronicles 16:34

About the Author

Mary AJ is a profoundly committed woman of faith, widely recognized for her devotion to God and her role as a spiritual mentor. As a proud mother of four and grandmother of eight and three great-grandchildren, she has also extended her care and guidance to over two hundred spiritual women and children, inspiring them to grow closer to God and live faith-filled lives.

Mary AJ has devoted her life to disseminating the Word of God, assisting women in healing from past traumas, and inspiring them to discover hope within their spiritual journeys. Her ministry is characterized by creating a safe and welcoming environment and promoting opportunities for transformation and renewal. She extends compassion and understanding to all individuals she meets.

With a genuine commitment to uplifting others, Mary AJ travels extensively throughout the United States and internationally. She delivers impactful messages centered on faith, healing, and hope. Her speaking engagements motivate individuals to embrace the gospel's transformative power, leaving a profound and lasting impression on *all who attend.*

Made in the USA
Middletown, DE
30 January 2025

70594643R00064